VENEZUELA 2016 HUMAN RIGHTS REPORT

EXECUTIVE SUMMARY

Venezuela is formally a multiparty, constitutional republic, but for more than a decade, political power has been concentrated in a single party with an increasingly authoritarian executive exercising significant control over the legislative, judicial, citizen, and electoral branches of government. Nicolas Maduro won the presidency in 2013 by a 1.5-percent margin amid allegations of pre- and post-election fraud, including government interference, the use of state resources by the ruling party, and voter manipulation. The opposition won in a landslide control of the National Assembly in the December 2015 legislative elections, but the executive branch exercised extensive influence over the judiciary to secure favorable decisions from the Supreme Tribunal of Justice that undermined the National Assembly's autonomy, ignored the separation of powers, and enabled the president to govern through a series of emergency decrees. The ruling United Socialist Party (PSUV) subsequently thwarted opposition efforts to recall the President under terms laid out by the constitution, and gubernatorial elections slated for December 2016 were summarily postponed.

Civilian authorities maintained effective, though politicized, control over the security forces.

Principal human rights abuses reported during the year included systematic, politicized use of the judiciary to undermine legislative branch action, and intimidate and selectively prosecute critics; indiscriminate police action against civilians leading to widespread arbitrary detentions, unlawful deprivation of life, and torture; and government curtailment of freedom of expression and of the press. The government arrested and imprisoned opposition figures and showed little respect for judicial independence or generally did not permit judges to act according to the law without fear of retaliation. At times the government blocked media outlets and harassed and intimidated privately owned television stations, other media outlets, and journalists throughout the year using threats, fines, property seizures, arrests, criminal investigations, and prosecutions.

Nongovernmental organizations (NGOs), the media, and government agencies reported extrajudicial killings by police and security forces; torture and other cruel, inhuman, or degrading treatment; harsh and life-threatening prison conditions and lack of due process rights that contributed to widespread violence, riots, injuries, and deaths in prisons; inadequate juvenile detention centers; corruption and impunity in the police; arbitrary arrests and detentions; abuse of political prisoners; interference with privacy rights; lack of government respect for freedom of assembly; lack of protection for Colombian migrants; corruption at all levels of government; threats against domestic NGOs; violence against women; employment discrimination based on political preference; and restrictions on workers' right of association.

The government sometimes took steps to punish lower-ranking government officials who committed abuses, but there were few investigations or prosecutions of senior government officials. Impunity remained a serious concern in the security forces.

Section 1. Respect for the Integrity of the Person, Including Freedom from:

a. Arbitrary Deprivation of Life and other Unlawful or Politically Motivated Killings

Although the government did not release statistics on extrajudicial killings, NGOs reported that national, state, and municipal police entities, as well as the armed forces and government-supported paramilitary groups, known as "colectivos," carried out such killings during the year.

There was also no official information available on the number of public officials prosecuted or sentenced to prison for involvement in extrajudicial killings, which, in the case of killings committed by police, were often classified as "resistance to authority." The NGO Committee for the Families of Victims of February-March 1989 (COFAVIC) continued to report there was no publicly accessible national registry of reported cases of extrajudicial killings.

COFAVIC reported that in 2015 there were 1,396 alleged extrajudicial killings committed by members of security forces, a 37-percent increase over 2014. The national police Scientific, Penal, and Criminal Investigative Corps (CICPC) reportedly committed 30 percent of the acts, with others committed by regional and municipal police. According to NGOs, prosecutors occasionally brought cases against such perpetrators, but prosecutions often resulted in light sentences, and convictions often were overturned on appeal.

COFAVIC reported cases in all 23 states and the national capital district of what it defined as extrajudicial killings committed by elements within local and state police forces. COFAVIC reported these elements systematically and arbitrarily detained and killed individuals (mainly young men from lower social classes) without any recourse to proper investigation by the government.

The government continued its nationwide anticrime strategy begun in 2015, the Operation for the Liberation and Protection of the People (OLP), characterized by large-scale raids conducted by hundreds of government security agents in neighborhoods allegedly harboring criminals. These operations often resulted in the deaths of suspected criminals. The NGO Venezuela Program for Education/Action on Human Rights (PROVEA) reported that 245 persons were killed during OLP security exercises in 2015.

The government continued to prosecute individuals connected with the 1989 killings in Caracas known as the "Caracazo," in which the Public Ministry estimated 331 individuals died, and the 1988 El Amparo massacre, in which government security forces allegedly killed 14 persons.

On November 27, the state prosecutor stated the government would charge 11 members of the military for responsibility in the death of 12 civilians following a security raid in October in the coastal state of Miranda. The Defense Ministry declared that it condemned the deaths, as did the National Assembly in a rare, unanimous resolution.

b. Disappearance

There were no substantiated reports of politically motivated disappearances.

c. Torture and Other Cruel, Inhuman, or Degrading Treatment or Punishment

Although the constitution states no person shall be subjected to cruel, inhuman, or degrading punishment, there were credible reports security forces tortured and abused detainees.

There were no reports of any government officials being charged under the law that states an agent or public official who inflicts pain or suffering--whether physical or mental--on another individual to obtain information or a confession, or seeks to punish an individual for an act the individual has committed, may be imprisoned for a maximum of 25 years, dismissed from office, and barred from holding public office for a maximum of 25 years. Prison and detention center officials who commit torture may face a maximum of five years in prison and a maximum fine of 53.5 million bolivars (BsF) ($5.3 million at the official rate, or $80,666 at the secondary Dicom exchange rate as of December 1). The law also includes mechanisms for reparations to victims and their families and creates a special National Commission for Torture Prevention composed of several government ministries.

The Office of the Human Rights Ombudsman and the Public Ministry did not publish statistics regarding allegations of torture by police during the year. Several NGOs detailed cases of widespread torture and "cruel, inhumane, and degrading treatment." The Venezuelan NGO Foro Penal documented more than 138 cases of torture in the country between February 2014 and May 2015. Foro Penal maintained that hundreds of cases were not reported to government institutions because of victims' fear of reprisal. NGOs detailed reports from detainees whom authorities allegedly sexually abused, threatened with death, and forced to spend hours on their knees in detention centers.

Human rights groups reported that the government continued to influence the prosecutor general and the public defender to conduct investigations selectively and subjectively. No data was available on investigations, prosecutions, or convictions in cases of alleged torture.

Press and NGO reports of beatings and humiliating treatment of suspects during arrests were common and involved various law enforcement agencies and the military. Torture and other cruel, inhuman, or degrading treatment or punishment of prisoners were reported during the year. Two common methods of cruel treatment were the denial of medical care by prison authorities and the remanding of prisoners to long periods in solitary confinement. In the case of opposition leader Leopoldo Lopez, family members stated that prison authorities held him in solitary confinement for much of his imprisonment, subjected him to strip searches multiple times daily, denied him visitation rights, and occasionally deprived him of reading and writing material. Prison officials also subjected visiting family members to humiliating strip searches.

The NGO Foro Penal reported multiple instances of political prisoners denied adequate medical treatment while in government custody. Foro Penal noted instances where detainees were transferred to a medical facility, where instead of receiving treatment, they were interrogated by security officials.

Prison and Detention Center Conditions

Most prison conditions were harsh and life threatening due to insufficient numbers of staff, who were also poorly trained and allegedly corrupt; weak security; deteriorating infrastructure; severe overcrowding; lack of adequate medical care; and shortages of food and potable water. Armed gangs effectively controlled some prisons in which they were incarcerated.

<u>Physical Conditions</u>: The Ministry of Penitentiary Services reported there were 50,791 inmates in the country's 58 prisons and penitentiaries and an estimated of 33,000 inmates in police station jails. According to the NGO Venezuelan Observatory for Prisons (OVP), the capacity for penitentiaries was 22,459 inmates, and for police station jails, the capacity was for 5,000 inmates. Overcrowding was 126 percent for penitentiaries and 560 percent for police station jails on average, although the OVP noted that in some jails the overcrowding ranged from 800 to 1,200 percent.

According to OVP reports, records for detainees were not properly maintained and often featured incomplete information. Official figures taken from the Penitentiary Services Ministry's 2015 annual report estimated 31,503 pretrial detainees and 17,374 convicted prisoners were held in the same facilities. Authorities assigned another 265 individuals to work detachment programs and held 522 individuals in police station facilities not fit to serve as detention centers. Women (2,629 inmates) and men (48,162 inmates) generally were held in separate prison facilities. There was only one penitentiary exclusively for women, and female prisoners in other detention centers were held in annexes or separate women's departments in otherwise male-only prisons. Security forces and law enforcement authorities often held minors together with adults, even though separate facilities existed. Because institutions were filled to capacity, hundreds of children accused of infractions were confined in juvenile detention centers where they were reportedly crowded into small, unsanitary cells.

The CICPC and police station jails and detention centers also were overcrowded, causing many police station offices to be converted into makeshift prison cells. Prisoners reportedly took turns sleeping on floors and office chairs, and sanitation facilities were inadequate or nonexistent. In the temporary detention facility in the downtown Caracas Zona 7 police station, a reported 700 detainees awaiting transport to prisons were held in a facility built for 70. On January 21, Mayor Ramon Muchacho of the Caracas municipality of Chacao declared that Chacao Police Department detention centers were operating at 300 percent of capacity, and temporary facilities were being used for long-term detention due to the lack of space in national penitentiaries. Muchacho highlighted that temporary detention centers lacked the infrastructure and security conditions to handle long-term imprisonment, and that overcrowding limited the fundamental rights for prisoners to receive visitors and legal counsel.

The National Guard and the Ministry of Interior, Justice, and Peace have responsibility for prisons' exterior and interior security, respectively. The government failed to provide adequate prison security. The OVP estimated a staffing gap of 90 percent for prison security personnel, with only one guard for every 100 inmates, instead of one every 10 as recommended by international standards. The OVP reported 309 prisoner deaths and 1,709 serious injuries in 2014. Most deaths and injuries resulted from prisoner-on-prisoner violence, riots, fires, and generally unsanitary and unsafe conditions. On August 3, seven prisoners at Alayon prison in Maracay died and approximately 60 individuals, three of them police officers, were severely injured when subjects riding motorcycles threw five grenades into the facility. The media reported that after the incident an undetermined number of inmates escaped from the prison.

During the year numerous prison riots resulted in inmate deaths and injuries. On January 11, 50 inmates took 40 persons hostage, including prison guards and staff and visiting family members, in Coro Penitentiary while protesting against food shortages and inadequate health care. The riot lasted for 55 hours and led to 11 injuries, 10 of them prison guards. On August 10, gangs rioted at the San Felix police station jail, leaving two inmates dead and 11 injured. Gang-related violence and alleged extortion by guards and inmates was fueled by trafficking in arms and drugs. NGOs, human rights lawyers, and the press frequently claimed prison gang leaders, rather than government authorities, controlled the penitentiaries and were able to lead organized crime networks based outside the prison system.

On July 15, a new law came into effect limiting cellphone and internet availability inside prisons to prevent inmates from using the technology to engage in criminal activity. The law was not implemented, however; inmates threatened a "full-scale war" if the government limited their ability to communicate.

The NGO A Window to Liberty (UVL) reported that authorities asked family members to provide nonperishable foods to prisoners at police station jails and the Fenix, Rodeo I, Rodeo II, Rodeo III, Yare III, and National Institute of Feminine Orientation penitentiaries due to inadequate provisioning of food by the prison administration. Lack of potable and running water in the 26 de Julio penitentiary led to gastrointestinal and skin diseases for large portions of the inmate population and prison staff.

The government restricted information regarding deaths in prisons from tuberculosis, HIV/AIDS, and other diseases, or lack of medical care. A study by the NGO Solidarity Action found prison rules regarding the classification of inmates resulted in the isolation of those with HIV/AIDS in "inadequate spaces without food and medical attention." The OVP reported a generalized lack of medical care, drugs, equipment, and physicians for prisoners, and reportedly inmates often received the same pills regardless of their symptoms. The OVP reported that due to inadequate nutrition plans and lack of potable water, stomach illnesses were common among inmates. According to the OVP, pregnant women lacked adequate facilities for their medical attention.

Administration: The government's recordkeeping on prisoners was inadequate. Prison authorities did not maintain accurate counts of inmates. According to press reports, the most recent accurate daily counts at the General Penitentiary of Venezuela and the La Planta Penitentiary occurred in 2009 and 2010, respectively.

The National Assembly released a report in May evaluating the use of funds by Minister Varela, noting that the Prisons Ministry had built only two new penitentiaries of 24 planned since 2012. In addition, the ministry's 2015 annual report indicated that the budget for prisons, managed by the National Penitentiaries Fund (FONEP), had been reduced by 86 percent from 2013 to 2015.

The Ministry of Penitentiary Services did not respond to any of the requests it received from the OVP, UVL, other human rights organizations, inmates, or families regarding inmates or investigations of the harsh conditions that led to hunger strikes or violent uprisings.

Prisoners and detainees generally had access to visitors, but in some cases prison officials harassed or abused visitors. Prison officials imposed significant restrictions on visits to political prisoners. The family of imprisoned opposition leader Leopoldo Lopez denounced mistreatment by prison guards when attempting to visit him in the Ramo Verde Military Prison, including being subjected to strip searches on both entry and exit from the facility.

Independent Monitoring: Human rights observers continued to experience lengthy delays and restrictions in accessing prisons and detention centers. Requests by the International Committee of the Red Cross (ICRC) to visit penitentiary centers and interview inmates in confidentiality have been rejected since 2013. More than 300 lay members from the Venezuelan Episcopal Conference of the Roman Catholic

Church volunteered in 40 prisons. Although prohibited from formally entering prisons, Catholic laity visited prisoners on family visitation days.

Improvements: In February the Ministry of Penitentiary Services announced closure of the San Antonio Prison in Nueva Esparta after a series of videos were released on social media showing inmates firing weapons to commemorate the death of prison gang leader "El Conejo," who was killed on January 24. Authorities moved 1,828 prisoners to other government penitentiaries. The ministry implemented educational programs for inmates, although reports from an NGO claimed enrollment was low.

d. Arbitrary Arrest or Detention

The constitution prohibits the arrest or detention of an individual without a judicial order and provides for the accused to remain free while being tried, but individual judges and prosecutors often disregarded these provisions. While NGOs such as Foro Penal, COFAVIC, the Institute for Press and Society (IPYS), Public Space, and PROVEA noted at least 2,000 open cases of arbitrary detentions, authorities rarely granted them formal platforms to present their petitions. Multiple individuals, including American citizens, were arbitrarily detained for extended periods without criminal charges.

In the weeks before a planned opposition rally on September 1, the government initiated a series of arbitrary detentions targeting opposition activists. On August 29, security forces arrested former student leader Yon Goicoechea for allegedly carrying explosives. Authorities held Goicoechea incommunicado for almost three days, and as of December 22, he remained in custody on politically motivated charges.

On September 3, independent journalist Braulio Jatar, a dual Venezuelan-Chilean citizen, was detained by Venezuelan authorities after reporting on an impromptu protest against President Maduro in Villa Rosa, Margarita Island. Jatar was charged with money laundering by a Venezuelan court, and as of December 22, he remained in the custody of the Bolivarian National Intelligence Service (SEBIN).

On September 19, SEBIN agents arrested Marco Trejo, Cesar Cuellar, and James Mathison without a warrant for producing a short video denouncing military repression. The government alleged the individuals committed a military offense because the video featured actors in military uniforms and charged the three under the military's code of conduct.

Role of the Police and Security Apparatus

The Bolivarian National Guard (GNB)--a branch of the military that reports to both the Ministry of Defense and the Ministry of Interior, Justice, and Peace--is responsible for maintaining public order, guarding the exterior of key government installations and prisons, conducting counternarcotics operations, monitoring borders, and providing law enforcement in remote areas. The Ministry of Interior, Justice, and Peace controls the CICPC, which conducts most criminal investigations, and SEBIN, which collects intelligence within the country and is responsible for investigating cases of corruption, subversion, and arms trafficking while maintaining its own detention facilities separate from those of the Ministry of Penitentiary Services. Police include municipal, state, and national police forces. Mayors and governors oversee municipal and state police forces. The Bolivarian National Police (PNB) reports to the Ministry of Interior, Justice, and Peace and had a reported 14,500 officers. According to its website, the PNB largely focused on policing Caracas' Libertador municipality; patrolling Caracas-area highways, railways, and metro system; and protecting diplomatic missions; the PNB maintained a minimal presence in seven of the country's 23 states.

Corruption, inadequate police training and equipment, and insufficient central government funding, particularly for police forces in states and municipalities governed by opposition officials, reduced the effectiveness of the security forces. There were continued reports of police abuse and involvement in crime, including illegal and arbitrary detentions, extrajudicial killings, kidnappings, and the excessive use of force.

Impunity remained a serious problem in the security forces. The Public Ministry is responsible for initiating judicial investigations of security force abuses. The Office of Fundamental Rights in the Public Ministry is responsible for investigating cases involving crimes committed by public officials, particularly security officials.

According to the Public Ministry's annual report for 2015, the Office of Fundamental Rights cited 13,911 specific actions taken to "process claims" against police authorities for human rights abuses and charged 959 with violations. The Office of the Human Rights Ombudsman did not provide information regarding human rights violations committed by police and military personnel, nor did the Attorney General's Office release data.

State and municipal governments also investigated their respective police forces. By law, national, state, and municipal police forces have a police corps disciplinary council, which takes action against security officials who commit abuses. The National Assembly also may investigate security force abuses.

During the year the government at both the local and national levels took few actions to sanction officers involved in abuses. According to the NGO Network of Support for Justice and Peace, the lack of sufficient prosecutors made it difficult to prosecute police and military officials allegedly involved in human rights abuses. In addition, NGOs reported the following problems contributed to an ineffective judicial system: long procedural delays, poor court administration and organization, lack of transparency in investigations, and impunity of government officials.

The National Experimental University for Security (UNES), tasked with professionalizing law enforcement training for the PNB and other state and municipal personnel, had centers in Caracas and five other cities. UNES requires human rights training as part of the curriculum for all new officers joining the PNB, state, and municipal police forces. Members of the PNB and state and municipal police also enrolled for continuing education and higher-learning opportunities as part of the Special Plan of Police Professionalization at UNES.

Societal violence remained high and continued to increase. The Public Ministry reported 19,453 homicides in 2015, a rate of 63.5 per 100,000 residents. The NGO Venezuelan Observatory of Violence estimated the rate to be higher, with 27,875 homicides, a rate of 90 per 100,000 residents. Criminal kidnappings for ransom were widespread in both urban centers and rural areas. Kidnappings included both "express kidnappings," in which victims were held for several hours and then released, and traditional kidnappings. The Public Ministry reported 793 cases of kidnapping or extortion in 2015. NGOs and police noted many victims did not report kidnappings to police or other authorities due to fear of retribution or lack of confidence in the police and that the actual occurrence was likely far higher.

Arrest Procedures and Treatment of Detainees

While a warrant is required for an arrest, detention is permitted without an arrest warrant when an individual is caught in the act of committing a crime or to secure a suspect or witness during an investigation. Police often detained individuals without a warrant. The law mandates that detainees be brought before a prosecutor within 12 hours and before a judge within 48 hours to determine the legality of the detention; the law also requires detainees be informed promptly of the charges against them. Authorities routinely ignored these requirements.

Although there is a functioning system of bail, it is not available for certain crimes. Bail also may be denied if a person is apprehended in the act of committing a crime or if a judge determines there is a danger the accused may flee or impede the investigation. The law allows detainees access to counsel and family members, but that requirement was often not met, particularly for political prisoners. The constitution also provides any detained individual the right to immediate communication with family members and lawyers who, in turn, have the right to know a detainee's whereabouts. A person accused of a crime may not be detained for longer than the possible minimum sentence for that crime or for longer than two years, whichever is shorter, except in certain circumstances, such as when the defendant is responsible for the delay in the proceedings.

Arbitrary Arrest: Foro Penal reported 5,853 cases of arbitrary detention between February 2014 and June 2016. Persons so detained claimed security personnel subjected them to inhuman and degrading treatment and in some cases torture.

Pretrial Detention: Pretrial detention was a serious problem. According to the OVP, approximately 79 percent of the prison population was in pretrial detention. According to the Supreme Court of Justice (TSJ), only 17 percent of trials concluded or reached sentencing. The NGO Citizen Observatory of the Penal Justice System attributed trial delays to the shortage of prosecutors and penal judges (4.7 penal judges per 100,000 inhabitants in 2010). The Public Ministry's 2015 annual report stated it had 346 prosecutors specializing in common crimes who processed more than 556,613 cases during the year.

Cases were often deferred or suspended when pertinent parties, such as the prosecutor, public defender, or judge, were absent. An automated scheduling calendar in use since 2013, which selected dates based on the availability of all pertinent parties and prohibited judges from scheduling more than 10 hearings per day, did not reduce the backlog. In some instances judges scheduled hearings six months from the start of the case.

According to the Public Ministry's 2015 annual report, the ministry pressed charges in 9.7 percent of the 556,000 cases involving common crimes. The ministry reported the closure of the remainder of the complaints but did not indicate final outcomes. Prisoners reported to NGOs that a lack of transportation and disorganization in the prison system reduced their access to the courts and contributed to trial delays.

On April 11, the Supreme Court ruled unconstitutional an amnesty law the National Assembly passed in March, which would have provided a framework to release political prisoners.

<u>Detainee's Ability to Challenge Lawfulness of Detention before a Court:</u> Individuals under detention may legally challenge grounds for their detention, but the processes were often delayed or tabled, and hearings were postponed, stretching trials for years. On many occasions the right to be judged in liberty for some offenders was not granted, and detainees were not allowed to consult with an attorney or to have access to their case records in order to challenge the detention. There are credible accounts that some detainees were placed on probation or under house arrest indefinitely and thus prevented from challenging their status by the threat of being sent back to detention.

e. Denial of Fair Public Trial

While the constitution provides for an independent judiciary, there was significant evidence the judiciary lacked independence. There were credible allegations of corruption and political influence throughout the judiciary. According to reports from the International Commission of Jurists (ICJ), between 66 and 80 percent of all judges had provisional appointments, and the TSJ Judicial Committee could remove them from office at will. Provisional and temporary judges, who legally have the same rights and authorities as permanent judges, allegedly were subject to political influence from the Ministry of Interior, Justice, and Peace and the attorney general to make progovernment determinations. The ICJ reported a lack of transparency and stability in the assignments of district attorneys to cases and the lack of technical criteria to assign district attorneys to criminal investigations. These deficiencies hindered the possibility of bringing offenders to justice and resulted in a 90-percent rate of impunity for common crimes and a higher percentage of impunity for human rights violation cases.

Trial Procedures

Defendants are to be considered innocent until proven guilty. The law requires that detainees be informed promptly of the charges against them, and the requirement was generally respected, although in high-profile cases the charges were often dubious, according to international human rights organizations. The law provides for open, public, and fair trials with oral proceedings for all individuals. Defendants have the right to consult with an attorney. Public defenders are provided for indigent defendants, but there continued to be a shortage of such attorneys. Defendants are not provided free interpretation as necessary from the moment charged through all appeals. According to the Office of the Human Rights Ombudsman, there were approximately 1,500 public defenders. COFAVIC and Foro Penal noted that the government pressured defendants in trials related to the 2014 student protests into utilizing public defenders instead of private defense attorneys with the promise of receiving more-favorable sentences. Additionally, several NGOs provided pro bono counsel to defendants.

While defendants and their attorneys have the right to access government-held evidence, access often was not allowed; in some instances, particularly in politically motivated cases, the court or prosecution did not allow defendants or their attorneys to access such information. Defendants may request no fewer than 30 days and no more than 45 days to prepare their defense. Defendants have the right to question adverse witnesses and present their own witnesses. By law defendants may not be compelled to testify or confess guilt. Defendants and plaintiffs have the right of appeal. The law extends these rights to all defendants.

Trial delays were common. Trials "in absentia" are permitted in certain circumstances, although opponents of them claimed the constitution prohibits such trials. The law also states a trial may proceed in the absence of the defense attorney, with a public defender that the court designates. The law gives judges the discretion to hold trials behind closed doors if a public trial could "disturb the normal development of the trial."

At the September 28 hearing of Judge Maria Lourdes Afiuni, witnesses refused to appear for the prosecution. The legal situation of Afiuni, accused of corruption and abuse of authority for her 2009 decision to conditionally release on limits, remained unresolved. Afiuni continued to be subject to protective measures in place since her release to house arrest in 2011 that mandate she may not leave the country, talk to the media, or use social media, although the law states that such measures may not last more than two years.

The law mandates municipal courts to handle "less serious" crimes, i.e., those carrying maximum penalties of imprisonment for less than eight years. Municipal courts may levy penalties that include three to eight months of community service. Besides diverting some "less serious" crimes to the municipal courts, this diversion also permits individuals accused of "lesser crimes" to ask the courts to suspend their trials conditionally in exchange for their admission of responsibility, commitment to provide restitution "in a material or symbolic form," community service, and any other condition imposed by the court.

The law provides that trials for military personnel charged with human rights abuses after 1999 be held in civilian rather than military courts. In addition, under the Organic Code of Military Justice, an individual may be tried in the military justice system for "insulting, offending, or disparaging the national armed forces or any related entities." NGOs expressed concern with the government's practice of trying civilians under the military justice system for protests and other actions not under military jurisdiction.

Political Prisoners and Detainees

The government used the judiciary to intimidate and selectively prosecute individuals critical of government policies or actions. The NGO Foro Penal reported that more than 100 political prisoners remained incarcerated as of November. An additional 1,998 individuals were subject to either restricted movement or precautionary measures. In late August security forces detained numerous political activists in the days preceding antiregime demonstration on September 1.

In some cases political prisoners were held in SEBIN installations or the Ramo Verde military prison without an explanation of why they were not being held in traditional facilities. Authorities have denied the ICRC access to these prisoners since 2013.

On June 19, National Guardsmen arrested opposition party (Voluntad Popular) activists Gabriel San Miguel and others at a highway checkpoint in Cojedes State. The men were carrying pro-opposition pamphlets and approximately $3,000 worth of local currency and were traveling to help collect signatures as part of the recall referendum petition drive. SEBIN held the two men in solitary confinement and reportedly interrogated them without legal counsel present. Cojedes Governor Erika Farias accused them of carrying money "to pay mercenaries of destabilization" and blamed them for lootings at local supermarkets. On June 22, authorities charged them with "inciting violence" and money laundering, which could carry a prison sentence of more than 15 years. Authorities released San Miguel, a Spanish-Venezuelan dual national, on September 9 and dropped all charges; the other person, a U.S.-Venezuelan dual national, was released October 18.

Metropolitan Caracas Mayor Antonio Ledezma, arrested in February 2015, remained under house arrest while awaiting trial for alleged participation in a conspiracy to topple the government.

On August 12, a Caracas appeals court upheld the September 2015 conviction of Popular Will (Voluntad Popular) party leader and former Caracas Chacao municipality mayor Leopoldo Lopez on four counts of public incitement, damage to property, fire damage, and association for conspiracy, in a trial that began in 2014. Lopez continued serving a maximum sentence of 13 years and nine months in prison in Ramo Verde Military Prison, where he was held in solitary confinement. The court also denied the appeals of codefendants Christian Holdack and Marco Coello. During the appeal proceedings, as during the previous trial, court officials refused defense lawyers' requests to allow the media to cover the proceedings and denied admission to international observers.

On August 27, SEBIN agents transferred former San Cristobal mayor Daniel Ceballos from house arrest back to prison, alleging that he had been planning to engage in "destabilizing acts" during a September 1 political demonstration. Authorities had remanded Ceballos to house arrest in August 2015. He continued to await trial on charges of civil rebellion dating to 2014 protests, charges that carry a maximum sentence of 25 years.

Civil Judicial Procedures and Remedies

While there are separate civil courts that permit citizens to bring lawsuits seeking damages, there are no procedures for individuals or organizations to seek civil remedies for human rights violations.

f. Arbitrary or Unlawful Interference with Privacy, Family, Home, or Correspondence

The constitution provides for the inviolability of the home and personal privacy, but the government generally did not respect these prohibitions. In some cases government authorities infringed on citizens' privacy rights by searching homes without judicial or other appropriate authorization, seizing property without due process, or interfering in personal communications.

Beginning in August 2015, President Maduro declared 60-day "states of exception" in 23 municipalities bordering Colombia in Zulia, Tachira, Apure, and Amazonas states, thereby suspending the constitutional requirement for authorities to obtain a court order prior to entering a private residence or violating the secrecy of a person's private communications, among other constitutional rights. These states of exception continued throughout the year.

Section 2. Respect for Civil Liberties, Including:

a. Freedom of Speech and Press

The law provides for freedom of speech and press, but the combination of laws and regulations governing libel and media content, as well as legal harassment and physical intimidation of individuals and the media, resulted in significant repression of these freedoms. National and international groups, such as the Inter-American Commission on Human Rights (IACHR), the UN Human Rights Committee, Freedom House, the Inter American Press Association, Reporters without Borders, and the Committee to Protect Journalists, condemned or expressed concern over government efforts throughout the year to restrict press freedom and create a climate of fear and self-censorship.

Freedom of Speech and Expression: The law makes insulting the president punishable by six to 30 months in prison without bail, with lesser penalties for insulting lower-ranking officials. Comments exposing another person to public contempt or hatred are punishable by prison sentences of one to three years and fines. PSUV officials threatened violence against opposition figures and supporters, in particular leading up to the opposition's September 1 march.

Press and Media Freedoms: The law provides that inaccurate reporting that disturbs the public peace is punishable by prison terms of two to five years. The requirement that the media disseminate only "true" information was undefined and open to politically motivated interpretation. The Office of the UN High Commissioner for Human Rights (OHCHR) issued a statement in August expressing serious concern over the continuing erosion of media freedom.

The law prohibits all media from disseminating messages that incite or promote hate or intolerance for religious, political, gender-related, racial, or xenophobic reasons; incite, promote, or condone criminal acts; constitute war propaganda; foment anxiety in the population or affect public order; do not recognize legitimate government authorities; incite homicide; or incite or promote disobedience to the established legal order. Penalties range from fines to the revocation of licenses.

Despite such laws, President Maduro and the ruling PSUV used the nearly 600 government-owned or-controlled media outlets to insult and intimidate the political opposition throughout the year. Maduro regularly referred to Miranda state governor Henrique Capriles using homosexual slurs on live television, while PSUV First Vice President Diosdado Cabello used his weekly television program to bully journalists and media outlets.

The law declares telecommunications a "public interest service," thereby giving the government greater authority to regulate the content and structure of the radio, television, and audiovisual production sectors. The law provides that the government may suspend or revoke licenses when it judges such actions necessary in the interests of the nation, public order, or security. The law empowers the government to impose heavy fines and cancel broadcasts for violations of its norms; the National Telecommunications Commission (CONATEL) oversees the law's application.

The government introduced legal actions against high-profile independent media outlets *Tal Cual*, *El Nacional*, *El Nuevo Pais*, *La Patilla*, and Globovision.

The government's economic policies made it difficult for newspapers to access foreign currency, preventing many newspapers from purchasing critical supplies and equipment necessary for day-to-day business operations. Items that must be imported included ink, printing plates, camera equipment, and especially newsprint. As the government prevented newspapers from purchasing foreign currency, media companies were forced to buy newsprint from the government-run Alfredo Maneiro Editorial Complex, the only company allowed by the government to import it. Consequently, nearly every newspaper in the country reduced pages and news content in an attempt to conserve paper. On March 16, *El Carabobeno* stopped printing daily newspapers after 82 years in operation, the latest nongovernment-owned media outlet to cease production due to lack of access to dollars to purchase newsprint from the government.

The NGO Public Space reported 144 cases of violations of freedom of expression between January and June, defined as the "obstruction, impediment, or criminalization of the search, receipt, and distribution of information by the media," noting an increasing trend. The most common violations were aggressions against journalists and censorship. State-owned and state-influenced media provided almost continuous progovernment programming. In addition private and public radio and television stations were required to transmit mandatory nationwide broadcasts throughout the year. According to the online tracking program Citizens Monitoring, run by the civil society network Legislative Monitor, between January and September the government implemented more than 100 hours of national "cadenas" featuring President Maduro, interrupting regular broadcasts. Both Maduro and other ruling-party officials utilized mandatory broadcast time to campaign for progovernment candidates. Opposition candidates generally did not have access to media broadcast time.

The law requires practicing journalists to have journalism degrees and be members of the National College of Journalists, and it prescribes jail terms of three to six months for those practicing the profession illegally. These requirements are waived for foreigners and opinion columnists.

<u>Violence and Harassment</u>: Senior national and state government leaders continued to harass and intimidate privately owned and opposition-oriented television stations, media outlets, and journalists by using threats, property seizures, administrative and criminal investigations, and prosecutions. Government officials, including the president, used government-controlled media outlets to accuse private media owners, directors, and reporters of fomenting antigovernment destabilization campaigns and coup attempts.

IPYS reported 12 assaults on media offices from January to August. In two separate incidents in August, unidentified assailants threw feces at *El Nacional*'s Caracas headquarters and shot bullets at the offices of *Diario de los Andes* in Trujillo. According to statistics taken from an *El Carabobeno* special report, 34 percent of journalists claimed to have been harassed by government officials.

IPYS recorded at least 17 cases of journalists arbitrarily detained from January to August. On September 3, SEBIN agents detained *Reporte Confidencial* editor and Chilean-Venezuelan dual national Braulio Jatar for disseminating video of residents of Villa Rosa, Nueva Esparta, banging pots and pans in protest during President Maduro's visit to their community. Authorities charged Jatar with money laundering and using the proceeds to finance terrorism against the Maduro administration. As of December 22, Jatar remained in state custody.

Government officials also harassed foreign journalists working within the country. On August 31, immigration officials detained and deported a *Miami Herald* journalist despite having permitted him entry into the country the day before to cover planned opposition protests. Reporters from *The Washington Post*, ABC, Al-Jazeera, *Le Monde*, National Public Radio, and Colombia's Caracol Radio and TV were also expelled or denied entry upon arrival in the country during the year.

Censorship or Content Restrictions: In its 2015 report, IPYS noted the government's preference for using legal proceedings, financial sanctions, and administrative actions against unfavorable news outlets instead of incurring the political cost of shutting down them down outright. Members of the independent media stated they regularly engaged in self-censorship due to fear of government reprisals. This resulted in many journalists posting articles to their personal blogs and websites instead of publishing them in traditional media. The NGO Public Space reported that in 2015 there were 47 cases involving censorship.

The government also exercised control over content through licensing and broadcasting requirements. CONATEL acted selectively on applications from private radio and television broadcasters for renewal of their broadcast frequencies. According to Nelson Belfort, former president of the Venezuelan Radio Chamber, and NGO reports, approximately 2,000 radio stations were in "illegal" status throughout the country due to CONATEL having not renewed licenses for most radio stations since 2007.

The government controlled a large portion of the country's businesses and paid for advertising only with government-owned or government-friendly media.

Libel/Slander Laws: Government officials engaged in reprisals against individuals who publicly expressed criticism of the president or government policy. On April 11, a judge sentenced David Natera, editor of independent newspaper *Correo del Caroni*, to four years in prison for criminal defamation due to his newspaper's investigation of corruption at a state-run mining company in Bolivar State. Natera remained free pending appeal but was prohibited from leaving the country and required to appear before court officials every 30 days. In addition, the judge fined Natera BsF 201,249 ($20,124, or $30.34 at the Dicom exchange rate as of December 1) and ordered the newspaper not to publish stories about the case. *Correo del Caroni* also faced civil penalties stemming from the defamation case, which could result in the confiscation of its office and printing press, according to a statement released by the NGO Public Space.

National Security: The law allows the government to suspend or revoke licenses when it determines such actions to be necessary in the interests of public order or security. The government exercised control over the press through the public entity known as the Strategic Center for Security and Protection of the Homeland (CESPPA), established in 2013, which is similar to the government entity Center for National Situational Studies (CESNA), established in 2010. CESNA and CESPPA have similar mandates and are responsible for "compiling, processing, analyzing, and classifying" both government-released and other public information with the objective of "protecting the interests and objectives of the state."

On May 13, Maduro declared the "state of exception," citing a continuing economic emergency, and granted himself the power to restrict rights guaranteed in the constitution. The 60-day emergency decree allowed the president to block any action he deemed could "undermine national security" or could "obstruct the continuity of the implementation of economic measures for the urgent reactivation of the national economy." According to Human Rights Watch, the "state of exception" negatively affected the right to freedom of association and expression. On September 23, the TSJ renewed President Maduro's decree of a "state of exception."

Nongovernmental Impact: Widespread violence in the country made it difficult to determine whether attacks on journalists resulted from common criminal activity or whether criminals or others targeted members of the media.

Internet Freedom

The executive branch exercised broad control over the internet through the state-run CONATEL. Free Access reported that CONATEL supported monitoring of private communications and persecution of internet users who expressed dissenting opinions online. According to media reports, users of social networks accused CONATEL of monitoring their online activity and passing identifying information to intelligence agencies, such as SEBIN. According to Free Access, CONATEL provided information to SEBIN, including internet protocol addresses, which assisted authorities in locating the users. Free Access cited arrests of Twitter users during the 2014 protests.

The law puts the burden of filtering prohibited electronic messages on service providers, and it allows CONATEL to order service providers to block access to websites that violate these norms and sanctions them with fines for distributing prohibited messages.

CONATEL's director William Castillo repeatedly declared in press statements that the government did not actively block websites. Castillo stated CONATEL's role was to enforce the law and prevent dissemination of illegal information or material unsuitable for children and adolescents. Nevertheless, the government continued to block internet sites that post dollar- and euro-to-bolivar currency exchange rates differing from the government's official rate. Government-owned internet service provider CANTV facilitated blockages. The government used Twitter hashtags to attain "trending" status for official propaganda and employed hundreds of employees to manage and disseminate official government accounts. At least 65 official government accounts used Twitter to promote the ruling PSUV party.

Intelligence agencies, which lacked independent oversight, conducted surveillance for political purposes. Courts relied on evidence obtained from anonymous "patriotas cooperantes" (cooperating patriots) to persecute perceived opponents of the government, and senior government officials used personal information gathered by cooperating patriots to intimidate government critics and human rights defenders.

CONATEL reported 53 percent of the population used the internet during the year and estimated that 16.2 million citizens connected to the internet five to seven days per week.

Academic Freedom and Cultural Events

There were some government restrictions on academic freedom and cultural events. University leaders and students alleged the government retaliated against opposition-oriented autonomous universities by providing government subsidies significantly below the annual inflation rate to those universities. Autonomous universities, which receive partial funding from the government, received considerably less than the total budgets they requested. Furthermore, budgetary allocations were based on figures not adequately adjusted for inflation and covered expenses only through March.

On May 18, progovernment gangs attacked student protesters at the University of the Andes (ULA) in Merida and set fire to the medical school after students took refuge inside.

On June 14, President Maduro instructed the Education Ministry to implement a new high school curriculum in 127 schools nationwide for the 2016-17 school year. Teachers' associations criticized the new standards as being a form of political indoctrination, noting the replacement of key subjects such as history and geography with "homeland and civic duties" courses.

b. Freedom of Peaceful Assembly and Association

Freedom of Assembly

The constitution provides for freedom of assembly, but the government significantly restricted it. The Law on Political Parties, Public Gatherings, and Manifestations and the Organic Law for Police Service and National Bolivarian Police Corps regulate the right to assembly. Human rights groups continued to criticize such laws that enable the government to charge protesters with serious crimes for participating in peaceful demonstrations. Ambiguous language in the laws also allowed the government to criminalize organizations that were critical of the government. Protests and marches require government authorization in advance and are forbidden within designated "security zones." The opposition held large peaceful protests in September and October.

As part of the "states of exception" in place throughout the year in municipalities bordering Colombia and imposed via the "Economic Emergency Decree," the government ordered the suspension of the constitutional right to meet publicly or privately without obtaining permission in advance, as well as the right to demonstrate peacefully and without weapons.

Security agencies did not routinely provide sufficient protection for protesters in public rallies or to political leaders sponsoring them. NGOs and political activists cited a widespread fear of repression due to the militarization of the country and the increasing activities of progovernment gangs, ("colectivos,") against demonstrations.

The government continued repressing protesters and their leaders. On September 3, authorities briefly detained 30 individuals on Margarita Island for heckling President Maduro, after scores of inhabitants protested food shortages by banging pots and pans.

Freedom of Association

The constitution provides for freedom of association and freedom from political discrimination, but the government did not respect these rights. Although professional and academic associations generally operated without interference, a number of associations complained the National Electoral Council (CNE), which is responsible for convoking all elections and establishing electoral dates and procedures, and the Supreme Court repeatedly interfered with their attempts to hold internal elections. On July 26, Jorge Rodriguez, the mayor of Libertador municipality in Caracas and PSUV party leader, called on the CNE to dissolve the Democratic Unity Roundtable (MUD) opposition coalition due to alleged fraud committed during its campaign to organize a recall referendum.

The president's May 13 "state of exception" decree called upon the Foreign Ministry to suspend international funding to NGOs when "it is presumed" that funding is used with "political purposes or for destabilization." Human Rights Watch pointed out that in a country where authorities routinely accused human rights defenders of destabilizing democracy, this order could effectively shut down or dramatically scale back the operations of NGOs that rely on foreign funding to work independently. As of December 1, there were no reports of the government implementing the threats contained in this decree.

c. Freedom of Religion

See the Department of State's *International Religious Freedom Report* at www.state.gov/religiousfreedomreport/.

d. Freedom of Movement, Internally Displaced Persons, Protection of Refugees, and Stateless Persons

The constitution provides for freedom of internal movement, foreign travel, emigration, and repatriation; however, the government did not respect these rights.

Abuse of Migrants, Refugees, and Stateless Persons: Beginning in August 2015 and continuing during the year, the government implemented OLP security measures and increased the presence of security forces in Tachira State on the Colombian border. Authorities deported more than 1,700 Colombians in early stages of operations, and at least 22,000 more left the country due to fear of security abuses or deportation, according to the UN Office for the Coordination of Humanitarian Affairs. According to Colombia's Ombudsman's Office, which investigated 700 cases of deportations, none of the interviewed deportees received a hearing in order to challenge their removal. Many deportees claimed to have had legal permits to live in Venezuela. More than 400 of the Colombians who returned to Colombia had either requested asylum or been granted refugee status by Venezuela, according to the Global Protection Cluster in Colombia.

With the refugee status determination process centralized at the National Refugee Commission (CONARE) headquarters in Caracas, asylum seekers waited as long as three years to obtain a final decision. During this period they had to continue renewing their documentation every three months to stay in the country and avoid arrest and deportation. While travelling to the commission, particularly vulnerable groups, such as women with young children, the elderly, and persons with disabilities, faced increased protection risks, such as arrest and deportation, extortion, exploitation, and sexual abuse by authorities at checkpoints and other locations.

In addition to arbitrary deportations, Colombians expelled from the country complained of abuses by security forces. The IACHR reported that many deported Colombians alleged Venezuelan security forces used excessive force to evict them from their homes, which were subsequently destroyed, and that security agents subjected them to physical abuse and forceful separation from their families.

While no official statistics were available, a women's shelter reported recurring problems with gender-based violence and trafficking of refugee women.

Also see the Department of State's annual Trafficking in Persons Report at www.state.gov/j/tip/rls/tiprpt/.

The government generally cooperated with the Office of the UN High Commissioner for Refugees (UNHCR) and other humanitarian organizations in providing protection and assistance to refugees, asylum seekers, and other persons of concern.

In-country Movement: Following the declaration of a localized "state of exception" in August 2015, the government suspended transit through the national territory, including across international borders, and closed the border with Colombia. In August 2016 the countries negotiated an agreement to reopen the border gradually.

The government deployed thousands of security forces to restrict access to Caracas in the days leading up a major opposition-organized rally on September 1. Citing public safety, the government also routinely shut down public transportation networks on days and in areas where the opposition attempted to hold political rallies.

Protection of Refugees

<u>Access to Asylum</u>: According to UNHCR, 98 percent of asylum seekers came from Colombia. UNHCR estimated there were approximately 167,000 Colombian citizens in need of international protection in the country. Most of the Colombians had not accessed procedures for refugee status determination, due to the inefficiency of the process. UNHCR reported only 6,843 persons legally recognized as refugees. The influx of individuals seeking international protection continued through the different border areas until August 2015, when the government began closing key border crossings between Tachira and Zulia states and Colombia as part of the "states of exception" and the OLP. The vast majority of such persons remained without any protection.

On January 12, the Office of the Human Rights Ombudsman and UNHCR signed an agreement to guarantee refugees' human rights. The agreement aimed to expand the presence of regional ombudsman offices in the border regions. On May 27, CONARE and UNHCR launched a joint program to better assist refugees' needs. The program was designed to provide for a more complete registry of refugees, including victims of human trafficking.

<u>Access to Basic Services</u>: Colombian asylum seekers without legal residency permits had limited access to the job market, education, and health systems. The lack of documentation created significant challenges to achieving sufficient protection and long-term integration.

Section 3. Freedom to Participate in the Political Process

The 1999 constitution, the country's twenty-sixth since independence, provides citizens the ability to change their government through free and fair elections, but government interference, electoral irregularities, and manipulation of voters restricted the exercise of this right. In January government agencies harassed or fired workers following the December 2015 legislative elections. In June the CNE made available online a database of identifying citizens who had signed a petition requesting a recall referendum against President Maduro. PSUV politicians later used the database to fire or engage in employment discrimination against public employees and to withhold subsidized food benefits under the newly created Local Committees for Supply and Production program.

Elections and Political Participation

<u>Recent Elections</u>: On December 6, 2015, nationwide legislative elections took place largely peacefully, and the government initially accepted the results. Opposition candidates won 112 seats in the 167-seat National Assembly, while ruling-party PSUV candidates took 55 seats, despite a process that heavily favored the ruling party. The government rejected international election observation by the Organization of American States but permitted an "accompaniment" mission by the Union of South American Nations. Domestic observers reported voting machine failures, ruling-party tents illegally close to the entrance of the polls, improper use of public resources (e.g., state oil company vehicles with campaign slogans and government buses transporting supporters to vote), and press intimidation. In response to losing control of the legislative branch of government for the first time since 1999, the PSUV mobilized to appoint to the Supreme Court 13 new justices and 21 new alternates loyal to the PSUV.

On December 30, 2015, this newly reconstituted TSJ blocked one ruling party deputy-elect and three opposition deputies-elect from Amazonas State from taking office, based on allegations of electoral fraud, a decision that deprived the opposition of its two-thirds super-majority in the legislature. On July 28, the National Assembly, ignoring the TSJ's decision, swore in the three affected opposition deputies-elect for the second time. The TSJ subsequently ruled that the National Assembly was in contempt and all of its actions and future actions were invalid. In accordance with agreements from the dialogue talks, on November 15, the three opposition deputies from Amazonas State submitted their resignations to Congress. The government subsequently called for new elections in Amazonas State for late December, but the TSJ's contempt ruling against the National Assembly stood.

On October 20, the CNE suspended a nationwide, constitutionally based recall referendum process against President Maduro; the CNE referred to allegations of fraud in brought by government supporters before several state-level criminal courts. The CNE also declined to organize constitutionally mandated elections in December for the country's 23 governorships.

<u>Political Parties and Political Participation</u>: Opposition political parties operated in a restrictive atmosphere characterized by intimidation, the threat of prosecution or administrative sanction on questionable charges, and very limited mainstream media access. On September 2, after a series of partisan decisions favoring the ruling PSUV, the TSJ annulled all actions taken by the opposition-dominated National Assembly because of its failure to comply with previous TSJ rulings.

Some political organizations reported their main activists and leaders were victims of harassment and violence by the government and progovernment groups.

Participation of Women and Minorities: No laws limit the participation of women and members of minorities in the political process. A 2015 regulation requires political parties to put forth gender-balanced slates of candidates for legislative elections. Women held 24 of the 167 seats in the legislature and nine of the more than 30 cabinet-level positions.

Section 4. Corruption and Lack of Transparency in Government

The law provides criminal penalties for corruption by government officials, but the government did not implement the law effectively. Some government officials explicitly acknowledged impunity for corruption as a major problem. The government frequently investigated and prosecuted its political opponents on corruption charges to harass, intimidate, or imprison them. The Public Ministry cited numerous examples of investigations, stemming largely from improprieties in the distribution and sale of price-controlled items and in government currency allocations.

Corruption: The government continued a campaign to combat corruption through fast-track authority and executive powers, but critics contended the government's efforts focused only on low- to mid-level public officials while targeting high-level opposition politicians. The campaign included enforcement against smuggling of goods carried out by private citizens as part of what the government calls the fight against the "economic war" waged by the political opposition and foreign governments. According to the NGO Transparency Venezuela, weak government institutions and a lack of transparency allowed public officials at all levels to participate in corrupt activity with impunity. The National Assembly conducted its own corruption investigations, including against Rafael Ramirez, former head of PDVSA and current Venezuela Permanent Representative to the United Nations. Although well- publicized, these activities yielded no results.

On August 17, a court sentenced two executives of the state-owned airline Conviasa to four and one-half years in prison for their involvement in an overpricing scheme.

Corruption was a major problem in all police forces, whose members were generally poorly paid and minimally trained. There was no information publicly available about the number of cases involving police and military officials during the year, although the Public Ministry publicized several individual cases against police officers for soliciting bribes and other corrupt activities.

In a June 14 report, Transparency Venezuela criticized the widespread practice of nepotism in the government and cited the example of Controller General Manuel Gallindo, who employed at least 13 close family members in his office.

Financial Disclosure: The law requires public officials, as well as all directors and members of the boards of private companies, to submit sworn financial disclosure statements. By law the Public Ministry and competent criminal courts may require such statements from any other persons when circumstantial evidence arises during an investigation. In 2015 (the most recent data available) the Public Ministry cited 19,562 complaints or grievances of corruption, leading to charges against 4,119 individuals.

Public Access to Information: Although the law provides for public access to government information, human rights groups reported the government routinely ignored this requirement. The law requires a government agency to respond to a petition within 20 days of filing. The agency must also notify the applicant within five days of any missing information needed to process the request. Government agencies are subject to sanctions if they do not respond to a request. If the agency rejects the petition, an individual may file another petition or appeal to a higher level within the government agency. The agency must respond to the appeal within 15 days. The Pro Access Coalition, composed of NGOs advocating for the right to access public information, released a study in 2013 noting the government ignored 94 percent of citizen petitions for information, a trend cited as continuing during the year.

Section 5. Governmental Attitude Regarding International and Nongovernmental Investigation of Alleged Violations of Human Rights

A variety of independent domestic and international human rights groups generally operated with some government restrictions. Major domestic human rights NGOs conducted investigations and published their findings on human rights cases. Government officials generally were not cooperative or responsive to their requests. Some domestic NGOs reported government threats and harassment against their leaders, staff, and organizations, in addition to government raids and detentions, but were able to publish dozens of reports during the year. NGOs played a significant role in informing citizens and the international community about alleged violations and key human rights cases.

NGOs asserted the government created a dangerous atmosphere for them to operate. PSUV First Vice President Diosdado Cabello used his weekly talk show to intimidate members of NGOs, including Public Space, PROVEA, and Foro Penal. Several organizations, such as the OVP, PROVEA, Foro Penal, and Citizen Control, reported threats to their staff, conducted electronically or sometimes in person. Human rights organizations claimed they were subject to frequent internet hacking attacks and attempts to violate their e-mail privacy.

The law prohibits domestic NGOs from receiving funds from abroad if they have a "political intent"--defined as those that "promote, disseminate, inform, or defend the full exercise of the political rights of citizens"--or that seek to "defend political rights." The government threatened NGOs with criminal investigations for allegedly illegally accepting foreign funds. Various government officials accused human rights organizations on national television and media of breaking the law by receiving funding from international donors.

For violations, the law stipulates monetary penalties, a potential five- to eight-year disqualification from running for political office, or both. The law defines political organizations as those involved in promoting citizen participation, exercising control over public offices, and promoting candidates for public office. Although there was no formal application or enforcement of the law, it created a climate of fear among human rights NGOs and a hesitancy to seek international assistance.

In addition to the restrictions placed on fund raising, domestic NGOs also faced regulatory limitations on their ability to perform their missions. The law includes provisions eliminating the right of human rights NGOs to represent victims of human rights abuses in legal proceedings. The law provides that only the public defender and private individuals may file complaints in court or represent victims of alleged human rights abuses committed by public employees or members of the security forces.

The United Nations or Other International Bodies: The government was generally hostile toward international human rights bodies and continued to refuse to permit a visit by the IACHR, which had not visited the country since 2002. The government withdrew from the Inter-American Convention on Human Rights in 2013, but the IACHR continues to receive complaints from citizens and civil society. The government also refused to grant access to the OHCHR to investigate the human rights situation. The IACHR, UNHRC, and other human rights bodies criticized the government's handling of human rights issues during the year, including a September 29 joint statement by 30 countries at the 33rd session of the UN Human Rights Council.

Government Human Rights Bodies: In its May report, the Global Alliance of Human Rights Institutions, an international organization of national human rights institutions, recommended downgrading the country's status and cited the Office of the Human Rights Ombudsman, also called the Public Defender, for its failure to respond impartially to cases of human rights abuses in 2014. On February 27, President Maduro approved the national Human Rights Plan for 2016-19. Several NGOs criticized the plan, saying that it was produced without consultation. Throughout the year the government gave the plan minimal attention.

The National Assembly's subcommission on human rights played an insignificant role in human rights debates.

Section 6. Discrimination, Societal Abuses, and Trafficking in Persons

Women

Rape and Domestic Violence: The law criminalizes rape, including spousal rape, making it punishable by a prison term of eight to 14 years. Cases often were not reported to police due to fear of social stigma and retribution, particularly in light of widespread impunity. There were no comprehensive or reliable statistics on the incidence of sexual violence, rape, prosecutions, or convictions. A man legally may avoid punishment by marrying (before he is sentenced) the person he raped. Women faced substantial institutional and societal prejudice with respect to reporting rape and domestic violence. The law allows authorities to consider alternative forms of punishment, including work release, for those convicted of various crimes, including rape, if they have completed three-quarters of their sentence.

The law criminalizes physical, sexual, and psychological violence in the home or community and at work. The law punishes perpetrators of domestic violence with penalties ranging from six to 27 months in prison. The law requires police to report domestic violence to judicial authorities and obligates hospital personnel to notify authorities when admitting patients who are victims of domestic abuse. Police generally were reluctant to intervene to prevent domestic violence and were not properly trained to handle such cases. Reportedly, police systematically sent battered women to the Public Ministry without receiving victims' complaints in cases where extreme physical violence was not visible. The law also establishes women's bureaus at local police headquarters and tribunals specializing in gender-based violence, and two-thirds of states had specialized courts. According to the Public Ministry's 2015 annual report, 69 prosecutors were responsible for dealing exclusively with crimes against women.

Violence against women continued to be a serious and underreported problem. There were 121,168 cases involving violence against women according to the Public Ministry's 2015 annual report, leading to charges in 19,816 cases. According to a report from Attorney General's Office during the first semester of the year, there were a reported 75 femicides, an increase of 57 percent compared with the same period in 2015.

Many advocates observed there was a lack of public awareness among women regarding resources and support available to prevent and combat domestic violence. The government offered some shelter and services for victims of domestic and other violence, but NGOs provided the majority of domestic abuse support services.

Sexual Harassment: Sexual harassment is illegal and punishable by a prison sentence of one to three years. The law establishes a fine between BsF 3,210 ($321, or $4.84 at the secondary Dicom exchange rate as of December 1) and BsF 6,420 ($642, or $9.68 at the Dicom rate) for employers convicted of sexual harassment. Although allegedly common in the workplace, sexual harassment cases were rarely reported.

Reproductive Rights: Couples and individuals have the right to decide the number, spacing, and timing of their children; manage their reproductive health; and have access to the information and means to do so, free from discrimination, coercion, and violence. According to UN estimates, the maternal mortality ratio was 95 deaths per 100,000 live births. The main causes of maternal death were hemorrhagic disorders, high blood pressure, and infections. Traditional contraceptives such as condoms and birth control pills were scarce and prohibitively expensive when available. Doctors offered intrauterine devices, but most women could not afford them and opted for sterilization. Some local hospitals offered "sterilization days," but many women had to wait for months for the procedure because there were limited places at state-led hospitals. Private clinics were extremely expensive, in some cases charging an estimated 12 times the monthly minimum wage.

<u>Discrimination</u>: Women enjoy the same legal status and rights as men under the constitution. Women and men are legally equal in marriage, and the law provides for gender equality in exercising the right to work. The law specifies that employers must not discriminate against women with regard to pay or working conditions. The law also prohibits the requirement of a pregnancy test to qualify for a job and provides six weeks of maternity leave prior to birth and a 20-week period of maternity leave after birth or an adoption, and prohibits an employer from firing either parent for two years after a birth or adoption. Fathers are provided 14 continuous days of paternity leave after the birth of a child. According to the Ministry of Labor and the Confederation of Workers, regulations protecting women's labor rights were enforced in the formal sector, although according to the World Economic Forum, women earned 36 percent less on average than men doing comparable jobs.

The law provides women with property rights equal to those of men, but women frequently waived these rights by signing over the equivalent of powers of attorney to their husbands.

Children

<u>Birth Registration</u>: Citizenship is derived by birth within the country's territory. According to the UN Children's Fund (UNICEF), 92 percent of children under five were registered at birth.

<u>Child Abuse</u>: According to UNICEF and NGOs working with children and women, child abuse, including incest, occurred but was rarely reported. According to a National Institute for Statistics survey, 5 percent of victims of sexual abuse were children. According to the most recent statistics from the Public Ministry, 67 specialized prosecutors were assigned to handle cases involving the protection of children. Although the judicial system acted to remove children from abusive households, the press reported public facilities for such children were inadequate.

<u>Early and Forced Marriage</u>: The legal minimum age for marriage is 18 for women and men, but with parental consent the minimum age is 16 for women and men.

<u>Sexual Exploitation of Children</u>: By law sexual relations with a minor under age 13 or an "especially vulnerable" person, or with a minor under age 16 when the perpetrator is a relative or guardian, are punishable with a mandatory sentence of 15 to 20 years' imprisonment. The law prohibits the forced prostitution and corruption of minors. Penalties range from three to 30 years' imprisonment in the

case of sex trafficking of girls; however, the law requires force, fraud, or coercion in its definition of sex trafficking of girls.

The law prohibits the production and sale of child pornography and establishes penalties of 16 to 20 years' imprisonment. There was no publicly available information regarding the number of investigations or prosecutions of cases involving the commercial sexual exploitation of minors or child pornography.

Displaced Children: Leading advocates and the press estimated that 10,000 children lived on the streets. Authorities in Caracas and several other jurisdictions imposed curfews on unsupervised minors to attempt to cope with this problem, but with institutions filled to capacity, hundreds of children accused of infractions, such as curfew violations, were confined in inadequate juvenile detention centers.

International Child Abductions: The country is a party to the 1980 Hague Convention on the Civil Aspects of International Child Abduction. See the Department of State's *Annual Report on International Parental Child Abduction* at travel.state.gov/content/childabduction/en/legal/compliance.html.

Anti-Semitism

There were reports of societal abuses or discrimination based on religious affiliation, belief, or practice, including anti-Semitism.

The Confederation of Jewish Associations in Venezuela (CAIV) estimated there were 9,000 Jews in the country. There were no confirmed reports of anti-Semitic acts by the government, but Jewish community leaders expressed concern about anti-Semitic statements made by high-level government officials, and they noted that many other anti-Semitic incidents occurred during the year. The government-sponsored website Aporrea.org often published editorials asserting Venezuelan Zionists were conspiring against the government. On February 15, El Hatillo Mayor David Smolansky denounced a break-in at his house, during which the vandals also left anti-Semitic graffiti. On May 1, the state-owned media outlet *Telesur* published an article accusing opposition National Assembly deputies of having ties to a right-wing Zionist conspiracy against Latin America.

Trafficking in Persons

See the Department of State's *Trafficking in Persons Report* at www.state.gov/j/tip/rls/tiprpt/.

Persons with Disabilities

The law prohibits discrimination against persons with physical and mental disabilities in education, employment, health care, air travel and other transportation, the judicial system, and the provision of other state services, but the government did not make a significant effort to implement the law, inform the public of it, or combat societal prejudice against persons with disabilities. The law requires that all newly constructed or renovated public parks and buildings provide access, but persons with disabilities had minimal access to public transportation, and ramps were almost nonexistent. Online resources and access to information were generally available to persons with disabilities, although access to closed-captioned or audio-described online videos for persons with sight and hearing disabilities was limited. Separately, leading advocates for persons with hearing disabilities lamented difficult access to public services due to a lack of government-funded interpreters in public courts, health-care facilities, and legal services, as well as a lack of other public accommodations.

The National Commission for Persons with Disabilities (CONAPDIS), an independent agency affiliated with the Ministry for Participation and Social Development, advocated for the rights of persons with disabilities and provided medical, legal, occupational, and cultural programs. The government developed a series of employment fairs to increase the number of persons with disabilities in formal employment sectors, an initiative to help companies meet the legal requirement for 5 percent of employees to be persons with disabilities. According to CONAPDIS, fewer than 20 percent of persons with disabilities who registered with government health programs were fully employed. The state-run Mission for the Children of Venezuela provided monthly subsidies of BsF 600 ($60, or $0.90 at the Dicom exchange rate as of December 1) to heads of households for each child or adult with disabilities they supported.

There were several NGOs dedicated to assisting persons with disabilities with employment, education, and quality of life. The University of Monteavila hosted a research institute focused on the education of persons with disabilities.

National/Racial/Ethnic Minorities

The constitution prohibits discrimination based on race. The law prohibits all forms of racial discrimination and provides for a maximum of three years' imprisonment for acts of racial discrimination. As mandated by law, signage existed outside commercial and recreational establishments announcing the prohibition against acts of racial discrimination. The National Institute against Racial Discrimination worked under the Interior Ministry but did not have its own website or public information portal.

Indigenous People

The law prohibits discrimination based on ethnic origin, and senior government officials repeatedly stated support for indigenous rights. The constitution provides for three seats in the National Assembly for deputies of indigenous origin to "protect indigenous communities and their progressive incorporation into the life of the nation." Citing allegations of voter fraud, the TSJ annulled the December 2015 election of Amazonas State's indigenous representative to the National Assembly. The decision left some indigenous communities without representation in the national legislature.

Many of the country's approximately 800,000 indigenous persons were isolated from urban areas; lacked access to basic health, housing, and educational facilities; and suffered from high rates of disease. The government included indigenous persons in its literacy campaigns, in some cases teaching them to read and write in their native language(s) as well as in Spanish.

NGOs and the press reported local political authorities seldom took account of indigenous interests when making decisions affecting indigenous lands, cultures, traditions, or allocation of natural resources. Indigenous persons called on the government to recognize lands they traditionally inhabited as territories belonging to each respective indigenous group. The National Land Demarcation Commission, charged with implementing a land demarcation agreement reached after a violent 2008 land invasion, provided land titles in several communities, but indigenous groups continued to call for faster implementation of the demarcation process.

Indigenous groups regularly reported violent conflicts with miners and cattle ranchers over land rights. On February 12, Yarabana indigenous group leader Benjamin Perez denounced a violent attack committed against members of his group by illegal miners in Amazonas State.

There were reports of harassment, attacks, and forced evictions against indigenous people living in areas included as part of government mining concessions.

Border disputes with Colombia affected indigenous groups living in border regions. The government insisted the border closures, begun in August 2015 and lifted in August 2016, were necessary to eradicate contraband and violence in the region. One media outlet estimated 600,000 Wayuu families lived on both sides of the border. While the president proclaimed indigenous persons on the border could cross freely, there were many reported cases in which indigenous groups were restricted.

Acts of Violence, Discrimination, and Other Abuses Based on Sexual Orientation and Gender Identity

The constitution provides for equality before the law of all persons and prohibits discrimination based on "sex or social condition," but it does not explicitly prohibit discrimination based on sexual orientation or gender identity. According to a TSJ ruling, no individual may be discriminated against because of sexual orientation, but the ruling was rarely enforced. The media and leading advocates for the rights of lesbian, gay, bisexual, transgender, and intersex (LGBTI) persons noted that victims of hate crimes based on sexual orientation or sexual identity frequently did not report incidents and were often subjected to threats or extortion if they filed official complaints.

Since the law does not define a hate crime, no official law enforcement statistics reflected LGBTI-related violence. Most crimes against LGBTI persons were classified as "crimes of passion," not crimes of hate. The NGO Citizens' Association Against AIDS noted that in 28 of 29 cases of LGBTI persons who had been killed between 2004 and 2015, only one perpetrator was sentenced for a crime. Incidents of violence were most prevalent against members of the transgender community. Leading advocates noted that the media underreported most cases of LGBTI-related crime and law enforcement authorities did not properly investigate to determine the motives for such crimes. LGBTI experts also noted an estimated 6,000 same-gender families, with and without children, lacked legal protection.

Local police and private security forces allegedly prevented LGBTI persons from entering malls, public parks, and recreational areas. NGOs reported the government systematically denied legal recognition to transgender and intersex persons by preventing them from obtaining identity documents required for accessing education, employment, housing, and health care. This vulnerability often led transgender and intersex persons to become victims of human trafficking or prostitution.

Psychological, verbal, and physical abuses towards the LGBTI community were common practice in schools and universities, according to leading advocates. No laws or policies protect LGBTI persons against bullying. As a result, according to NGOs, LGBTI students had a higher dropout rate than heterosexual students.

HIV and AIDS Social Stigma

The law provides for the equal rights of persons with HIV/AIDS and their families. Nevertheless, leading advocates alleged discrimination against persons with HIV/AIDS.

Section 7. Worker Rights

a. Freedom of Association and the Right to Collective Bargaining

The law provides that all private- and public-sector workers (except armed forces members) have the right to form and join unions of their choice, and it provides for collective bargaining and the right to strike. The law, however, places several restrictions on these rights, and in practice, the government deployed a variety of mechanisms to undercut the rights of independent workers and unions. Minimum membership requirements for unions differ based on the type of union. Forming a company union requires a minimum of 20 workers; forming a professional, industrial, or sectoral union in one jurisdiction requires 40 workers in the same field; and forming a regional or national union requires 150 workers. Ten persons may form an employees association, a parallel type of representation the government endorses and openly supports.

The law prohibits "any act of discrimination or interference contrary to the exercise" of workers' right to unionize. The law requires that all unions must provide the Ministry of Labor a membership roster that includes the full name, home address, telephone number, and national identification number for each union member. The ministry reviews the registration and determines whether the union fulfilled all requirements. Unions must submit their registration by December 31 of the year the union forms; if not received by the ministry or if the ministry considers the registration unsatisfactory, the union is denied the ability legally to exist. The law also requires the presence of labor inspectors to witness and legitimize unions' decisions before the Ministry of Labor. The International Labor Organization (ILO) raised concerns about the ministry's refusal to register trade union organizations.

Under the law employers may negotiate a collective contract only with the union that represents the majority of their workers. Minority organizations may not jointly negotiate in cases where no union represents an absolute majority. The law also places a number of restrictions on unions' ability to administer their activities. For example, the CNE has the authority to administer internal elections of labor unions, federations, and confederations. By law elections must be held at least every three years. If CNE-administered and -certified elections are not held within this period, the law prohibits union leaders from representing workers in negotiations or engaging in anything beyond administrative tasks. The ILO repeatedly found cases of interference by the CNE in trade union elections and called since 1999 to delink the CNE from the union election process.

The law recognizes the right of all public- and private-sector workers to strike, subject to conditions established by law. By law workers participating in legal strikes receive immunity from prosecution, and their time in service may not be reduced by the time engaged in a strike. The law requires that employers reincorporate striking workers and provides for prison terms of six to 15 months for employers who fail to do so. Replacement workers are not permitted during legal strikes. The law prohibits striking workers from paralyzing the production or provision of essential public goods and services, but it defines "essential services" more broadly than ILO standards. The ILO called on the government to amend the law to exclude from the definition of "essential services" activities "that are not essential in the strict sense of the term…so that in no event may criminal sanctions be imposed in cases of peaceful strikes."

The minister of labor and social security may order public- or private-sector strikers back to work and submit their disputes to arbitration if the strike "puts in immediate danger the lives or security of all or part of the population." Other laws establish criminal penalties for the exercise of the right to strike in certain circumstances. For example, the law prohibits and punishes with a five- to 10-year prison sentence anyone who "organizes, supports, or instigates the realization of activities within security zones that are intended to disturb or affect the organization and functioning of military installations, public services, industries and basic [mining] enterprises, or the socioeconomic life of the country." In addition, the law provides for prison terms of two to six years and six to 10 years, respectively, for those who restrict the distribution of goods and for "those…who develop or carry out actions or omissions that impede, either directly or indirectly, the production, manufacture, import, storing, transport, distribution, and commercialization of goods."

The government restricted the freedom of association and the right to collective bargaining through administrative and legal mechanisms. Organized labor activists reported that the annual requirement to provide the Ministry of Labor a membership roster was onerous and infringed on freedom of association; they alleged the ministry removed member names from the rosters for political purposes, particularly if members were not registered to vote with the CNE. Labor leaders also criticized the laborious and costly administrative process of requesting CNE approval for elections and subsequent delays in the CNE's recognition of such union processes. Additionally, there reportedly was a high turnover of Ministry of Labor contractors resulting in a lack of timely follow-through on union processes.

Labor unions in both the private and public sectors noted long delays in obtaining CNE concurrence to hold elections and in receiving certification of the election results, which hindered unions' ability to bargain collectively.

The TSJ suspended union elections for the Orinoco Iron Workers Union (Sintraferrominera) three days before the scheduled May 27 vote. The TSJ ruling criticized irregularities in the call for elections, but the media reported that a more likely reason for the suspension was the low support for the PSUV union leader running for re-election. The Venezuelan Unitary Federation of Oil Workers (FUTPV) for Venezuelan Petroleum (PDVSA) workers had scheduled elections for August, but the FUTPV president, who had been due to run for re-election since 2014, again postponed the vote. According to potential opponent Jose Boadas, the government ordered a further delay to avoid "an imminent defeat" of the progovernment candidate and PSUV activist Wills Rangel.

According to PROVEA, "large sectors of national, state, and municipal public administrations and an important number of state enterprises continued to refuse to discuss collective agreements." According to the Autonomous Front in Defense of Employment, Wages, and Unions (FADESS), there were more than 300 expired public-sector union contracts nationwide. Labor leaders reported the majority of unions that failed to negotiate collective agreements were in the public sector. The Model Contract for Public Administration, which covers approximately three million public workers, was last negotiated in 2004. President Maduro promised it would be finalized in 2013, but no further progress was made during the year. The government did not respond to at least two formal ILO requests for information about reports that the majority of collective bargaining agreements in the public sector had expired but continued to be applied, with the right to collective bargaining denied by authorities due to "overdue elections" (not convoking or concluding the electoral process).

The government continued to support many "parallel" unions, which sought to dilute the membership and effectiveness of traditional independent unions. In general these government-supported unions were not subject to the same government scrutiny and requirements regarding leadership elections. For example, the Socialist Bolivarian Workers' Central had not held elections since 2011, yet it was regularly accredited to participate in ILO meetings, including for the ILO International Labor Conference in Geneva in June. The government excluded from consideration other, independent union federations, including the Confederation of Venezuelan Workers, the General Confederation of Venezuelan Workers, Confederation of Autonomous Unions of Venezuela, and National Union of Workers (UNETE). The ILO expressed continuing concern that the government did not consult with representative worker organizations or accredit their members to the ILO conference. In contrast, the Labor and Trade Union Action Unit, an independent organization of labor federations and other labor groups and movements, was able to meet freely to coordinate interventions for the July meeting, analyze conclusions from the meeting, and discuss follow-up actions.

According to the labor group FADESS, the ministry did not send labor inspectors to opposition-leaning union meetings to witness and legitimize unions' decisions, as required by law, thus rendering moot decisions by many unions.

The government continued to refuse to adjudicate or otherwise resolve the cases of 19,000 employees of the state oil company, PDVSA, who were fired during and after the 2002-03 strike. The Ministry of Labor continued to deny registration to the National Union of Oil, Gas, Petrochemical, and Refinery Workers (UNAPETROL), a union composed of these workers. Union elections in the state steel conglomerate's workers' trade union were suspended in 2014, and the TSJ upheld the suspension in January 2015.

Union leaders in the construction sector were subject to violent attacks--some of which resulted in killings. The lack of effective investigations made determining the motives for such attacks difficult; NGOs alleged the killings were the result of rival attacks over contracts. According to OVCS and PROVEA, the government did not make arrests or prosecute anyone for most violent crimes, including those committed between and against union workers, and few were solved. PROVEA reported that fewer than 5 percent of the cases were investigated. The ILO requested the government establish a national tripartite committee on situations of violence and provide information on the findings of the investigations carried out by the national prosecutor appointed to investigate all cases of violence against trade union leaders and members.

Union leaders were also subjected to harassment and verbal attacks. For instance, on his weekly television show, the former National Assembly president Diosdado Cabello made accusations against leaders from FADESS and the National Association of Autonomous Workers, Entrepreneurs, and Small Business Persons. The ILO raised concerns about violence against trade union members and government intimidation of the Associations of Commerce and Production of Venezuela (FEDECAMARAS).

The OVCS 2015 report on labor conflicts released on May 2 noted there were 969 labor-related protests in 2015. The OVCS's data revealed that salary increases had been insufficient to offset the impact of high inflation, layoffs, and other deteriorating conditions for workers. The OVCS reported that during the first six months of the year, there were 624 labor rights-related protests related to increased pay and benefits, the need for collective bargaining agreements, and outsourcing and the integration of contract workers. According to media reports, the government blacklisted and punished union leaders and workers for peaceful protests demanding wage increases and better conditions at work.

In practice the concept of striking had been demonized since 2002 and periodically used as a political tool to accuse government opponents of coup plotting or other destabilizing activities. Legal provisions on the right to strike were used to target company management as well as labor leaders. Labor activists were charged under legal provisions on impeding the production, manufacture, import, storing, transport, distribution, and commercialization of goods, as well as under provisions for "instigation to commit a crime," "blocking public access," and restriction of the "right to work." According to some business managers, some union leaders had extraordinary power to cause the arrest and prosecution of business managers for actions that could be considered normal aspects of their jobs. Some companies, especially in the public sector, had multiple unions with varying degrees of allegiance to the ruling party's version of the "socialist revolution," which could trigger interunion conflict and strife.

A 2012 law set a May 7 deadline for the incorporation of all contract workers in both the public and private sectors into the companies for which they worked. (The largest number of contract workers is in the public sector.) The media reported concerns that this deadline was not met and that the status of a large percentage of workers was not regularized. While there were no official statistics, media sources estimated that 40 percent of the contractor force had been transitioned into formal positions.

On June 7, dozens of workers from the state-owned electric utility company Corpoelec went on a hunger strike to pressure the government to resume negotiations for a collective bargaining agreement, as well as to protest a prohibition of the right to assembly on Corpoelec premises imposed by Electricity Minister Luis Motta. The collective bargaining negotiations had been suspended since May 3. The secretary general of the Electric Workers Federation (FETRAELEC), Reynaldo Diaz, said the union submitted a proposal of terms for the collective bargaining agreement to Labor Minister Osvaldo Vera on May 9 and had not received a response. After the first six days of the hunger strike, some workers faced health complications, and the strike was halted. FETRAELEC representatives declared they would continue pressuring the government with protests and strikes until the collective bargaining agreement was signed.

b. Prohibition of Forced or Compulsory Labor

The law prohibits some forms of forced or compulsory labor but does not provide criminal penalties for certain forms of forced labor. The law prohibits human trafficking by organized criminal groups through its law on organized crime, which prescribes 20 to 30 years' imprisonment for human trafficking carried out by a member of an organized criminal group of three or more individuals. The organized crime law, however, fails to prohibit trafficking by any individual not affiliated with an organized criminal group and fails to prohibit trafficking men. Prosecutors could employ other statutes to prosecute such individuals. The law includes harsher penalties for imposing forced labor on minors. There was no comprehensive information available regarding the government's enforcement of the law.

On July 19, the Ministry of Labor published Resolution 9855 requiring public- and private-sector businesses to provide male and female workers for 60 to 120 days in order to increase agricultural production. Amnesty International criticized the resolution as effectively amounting to forced labor. The resolution noted that the government would pay workers their normal salary while they participated in the program and that workers would not be fired from their ordinary jobs. The government did not implement the resolution during the year.

There were isolated reports of children and adults subjected to forced labor, particularly in the informal economic sector, in domestic servitude (see section 7.c.), and of Cubans working in government social programs (such as the Mission Inside the Barrio) in exchange for the government's provision of oil resources to the Cuban government. Indicators of forced labor reported by some Cubans included chronic underpayment of wages, mandatory long hours, limitations on movement, and threats of retaliatory actions to the workers and their families if they left the program.

Also see the Department of State's *Trafficking in Persons Report* at www.state.gov/j/tip/rls/tiprpt/.

c. Prohibition of Child Labor and Minimum Age for Employment

The law sets the minimum employment age at 14 years. Children younger than 14 may work only if granted special permission by the National Institute for Minors or the Ministry of Labor. Such permission may not be granted to minors under the age for work in hazardous occupations that risk their life or health or could damage their intellectual or moral development, but according to the ILO, the government had not made publicly available the list of specific types of work considered hazardous. Children ages 14 to 18 may not work without permission of their legal guardians or in occupations expressly prohibited by the law, and they may work no more than six hours per day or 30 hours per week. Minors under 18 may not work outside the normal workday.

The law establishes fines on employers between BsF 6,420 ($642, or $9.68 at the Dicom exchange rate as of December 1) and BsF 12,840 ($1,284, or $19.36 at the Dicom rate) for each child employed under age 12 or for adolescents between 12 and 14 employed without proper authorization. Anyone employing children under age eight is subject to a prison term between one and three years. Employers must notify authorities if they hire a minor as a domestic worker.

The Ministry of Labor and the National Institute for Minors enforced child labor laws effectively in the formal sector of the economy but less so in the informal sector. No information was available on whether or how many employers were sanctioned for violations. The government also continued to provide services to vulnerable children, including street children, working children, and children at risk of working. There was no independent accounting of the effectiveness of these and other government-supported programs.

Most child laborers worked in the agricultural sector, street vending, domestic service, or in small to medium-size businesses, most frequently in family-run operations. There continued to be isolated reports of children exploited in domestic servitude, mining, forced begging, and commercial sexual exploitation of children (see section 6).

Also see the Department of Labor's *Findings on the Worst Forms of Child Labor* at www.dol.gov/ilab/reports/child-labor/findings/.

d. Discrimination with Respect to Employment and Occupation

The constitution prohibits employment discrimination for every citizen. Labor law prohibits discrimination based on age, race, sex, social condition, creed, marital status, union affiliation, political views, nationality, disability, or any condition that could be used to lessen the principle of equality before the law. No law specifically prohibits employment discrimination on the basis of sexual orientation, gender identity, or HIV/AIDS status. The media and NGOs, such as PROVEA and the Human Rights Center at the Andres Bello Catholic University, reported the government had a very limited capacity to address complaints and enforce the law in some cases and lacked political will in some cases of active discrimination based on political motivations.

On January 3, President Maduro signed a presidential decree to protect government workers and shield them against arbitrary dismissals until 2018. Nevertheless, there were numerous reports of public workers who voted for the opposition in the December 2015 parliamentary elections being fired for "counterrevolutionary" activities. The Food Production and Distribution agency (PDVAL) fired 34 workers in the weeks following the December election and posted a listing referring to the dismissed workers as "traitors." The decision to disclose their names appeared intended to publicly shame the dismissed workers, goad progovernment loyalists into harassing them, and discourage future antiregime political activities. According to the media, workers at several other government agencies reported harassment, threats of firing, and labor discrimination for political reasons following the December election. Both the Children's Foundation and a mayor's office in Tachira State received criticism for alleged discrimination toward opposition voters.

In May, PSUV First Vice President and National Assembly Deputy Diosdado Cabello publicly announced that opposition supporters working for the public administration should leave their positions. In June Cabello called on governors' offices, mayors' offices, and ministries to identify employees that did not support President Maduro. Other progovernment politicians threatened to take actions against those who signed a recall referendum petition against Maduro after the CNE publicly disseminated a complete listing of signatories in early June, stating that government supporters should not tolerate opposition supporters working "in the revolutionary government." Human Rights Watch reported in July that the National Tax Revenue Service (SENIAT) fired dozens of workers nationwide in apparent retaliation for supporting a recall referendum against Maduro. Other government agencies reportedly fired hundreds of other referendum supporters in similar circumstances. The Venezuelan National Petroleum Workers Federation announced on October 20 that PDVSA had rescinded the contracts of 2,000 temporary oil workers for political reasons.

e. Acceptable Conditions of Work

The government raised the monthly minimum wage four times between January and October 26, reflecting a 180-percent increase, bringing it to a total of BsF 27,000 ($2,700, or $40.72 at the Dicom exchange rate as of December 1). The minimum wage also included a nonsalary food ticket subsidy of BsF 64,000 ($6,400, or $96.53 at the Dicom rate), bringing the total monthly minimum wage to BsF 91,000 ($9,100, or $137.25 at the Dicom rate). According to the NGO Workers' Center for Documentation and Analysis, the monthly food basket for a family of five for September cost BsF 465,035 ($46,503, or $701.41 at the Dicom rate), or 7.1 times the minimum wage.

The law sets the workweek at 40 hours (35 hours for a night shift). The law establishes separate limits for "shift workers," who may not work more than an average of 42 hours per week during an eight-week period, with overtime capped at 100 hours annually. Managers are prohibited from obligating employees to work additional time, and workers have the right to two consecutive days off each week. Overtime is paid at a 50-percent surcharge if a labor inspector approves the overtime in advance and at a 100-percent surcharge if an inspector does not give advance permission. The law establishes that after completing one year with an employer, the worker has a right to 15 days of paid vacation annually. The worker has the right to an additional day for every additional year of service, for a maximum of 15 additional days annually.

The law provides for secure, hygienic, and adequate working conditions. Workplaces must maintain "protection for the health and life of the workers against all dangerous working conditions." The law obligates employers to pay workers specified amounts for workplace injuries or occupational illnesses, ranging from two times the daily salary for missed workdays to several years' salary for permanent injuries. Workers may remove themselves from situations that endanger health or safety without jeopardy to their employment.

The law covers all workers, including temporary, occasional, and domestic workers. Reportedly, there was some enforcement by the Ministry of Labor of minimum wage rates and hours of work provisions in the formal sector, but 40 percent of the population worked in the informal sector, where labor laws and protections generally were not enforced. The government did not enforce legal protections on safety in the public sector. According to PROVEA, while the National Institute for Prevention, Health, and Labor Security required many private businesses to correct dangerous labor conditions, the government did not enforce such standards in a similar manner in state enterprises and entities. There was no publicly available information regarding the number of inspectors or the frequency of inspections to implement health and safety, minimum wage, or hours of work provisions. Ministry inspectors seldom closed unsafe job sites. Employers may be fined between BsF 12,840 ($1,284, or $19.36 at the Dicom rate) and BsF 38,520 ($3,852, or $58.08 at the Dicom rate) for failing to pay the minimum wage or provide legally required vacation time. Employers are required to report work-related accidents within 24 hours or face fines between BsF 8,132 ($813, or $12.26 at the Dicom rate) and BsF 10,700 ($1,070, or $16.13 at the Dicom rate). There was no information on whether penalties were sufficient to deter violations.

Official statistics regarding workplace deaths and injuries were not publicly available.